Made in Ancient EGYPT

By Sue Adasiewicz

Scott Foresman
is an imprint of

PEARSON

Glenview, Illinois • Boston, Massachusetts • Chandler, Arizona •
Upper Saddle River, New Jersey

Photographs

Every effort has been made to secure permission and provide appropriate credit for photographic material. The publisher deeply regrets any omission and pledges to correct errors called to its attention in subsequent editions.

Unless otherwise acknowledged, all photographs are the property of Pearson Education, Inc.

Photo locators denoted as follows: Top (T), Center (C), Bottom (B), Left (L), Right (R), Background (Bkgd)

Opener: Building the Pyramids, Dear, Neville (b.1923)/Private Collection/©Look and Learn/Bridgeman Art Library; **1** ©Fridmar Damm/zefa/Corbis; **3** (TR, CR) ©DK Images, (BR) ©Gregor Schuster/zefa/Corbis, (L) ©Map Resources/Alamy; **4** ©Fridmar Damm/zefa/Corbis; **5** ©North Wind Picture Archives/Alamy Images; **6** Jupiter Images; **7** (Inset) Hulton Archive/Getty Images, (Bkgd) ©Iconotec/Alamy; **8** Building the Pyramids, Dear, Neville (b.1923)/Private Collection/©Look and Learn/Bridgeman Art Library; **9** (B) INTERFOTO Pressebildagentur/Alamy Images, (C) DEA/S. VANNINI /Getty Images, (T) ©Sandro Vannini/Corbis; **10** ©Peter Barritt/Alamy; **11** ©Dmitri Kessel/Time Life Pictures/Getty Images; **12** ©Sandro Vannini/Corbis; **13** ©Michael Nicholson/Corbis.

ISBN 13: 978-0-328-47281-9
ISBN 10: 0-328-47281-6

3 4 5 6 7 8 9 10 V010 13 12 11 10

The **civilization** of ancient Egypt began along the Nile River more than 5,000 years ago. Over the next 3,000 years, the ancient Egyptians succeeded in making advancements in many fields. Some of these improvements helped them travel, work, tell time, and count.

Ancient Egypt was located in northeast Africa in what is today the modern country of Egypt.

The ancient Egyptians used the stalks from the papyrus plant to make paper.

The ancient Egyptians used hieroglyphics, or picture writing.

The Nile River was the main transportation route in ancient Egypt. To make traveling on the river easier and faster, the ancient Egyptians fixed square sails to their boats.

The sails caught the wind, and the boats moved swiftly in the direction the wind blew.

The ancient Egyptians used water from the Nile River to **irrigate** their crops. They made a tool called a shadoof to help raise water from the river to the land. The water was dumped from the filled container into an irrigation canal.

The shadoof had a pole that went up and down like a seesaw. There was a container at one end and stone weights at the other.

Farmers in ancient Egypt improved the way they plowed the land. They used an ox-drawn plow to turn up the **fertile** soil. They attached a bar to the oxen's horns. Ropes went from the bar to the plow so the oxen could pull it.

The ox-drawn plow made farming easier.

The ancient Egyptians locks were similar to present-day tumbler locks.

To protect their homes against robberies, the ancient Egyptians made locks for their doors. The locks had movable pins. **Gravity** dropped the pins into a crossbar to lock the door. A key moved the pins to open the door.

It was important for farmers in ancient Egypt to know when to plant their crops. The ancient Egyptians used the cycles of the Nile River to make a calendar that divided a year into three seasons. Each season was four months long, with thirty days in each month.

During the flooding season, many farmers worked for the pharaoh, or king. They built pyramids and temples.

The Three Seasons of Ancient Egypt		
Inundation The Flooding Season	July - October 	The Nile River flooded the fields. No farming could be done.
Emergence The Growing Season	November - February 	The Nile River went down. Planting was done in the fertile soil.
Summer The Harvesting Season	March - June 	The full-grown crops were cut down. Repairs were made to the canals before the Nile flooded again.

Five days were added to the calendar at the end of the year. This made a year with 365 days. The extra days were used for feasting and celebrating.

The sun clock also showed the year's shortest and longest days.

The need to know the time of day led to advancements in clock-making. The ancient Egyptians used an **obelisk**, a four-sided stone pillar, to make a sun clock. As the sun moved across the sky, the obelisk cast shadows on the ground. The length of the shadows divided the day into morning and afternoon.

A water clock could be used at night. One of the oldest water clocks in existence was found in a pharaoh's tomb.

The ancient Egyptians also made water clocks. They poured water into a stone container that had sloping sides and a small hole in the bottom. As the water dripped at a steady rate through the hole, the water level went down. Markings on the inside of the container showed the passing of hours.

The ancient Egyptians made advancements in medicine. Their doctors did surgery and made medicines using herbs and minerals. They used honey and willow bark to keep germs out of wounds. Doctors even told people with breathing problems to inhale steam.

Ancient Egyptian doctors knew about the body's internal organs from the custom of embalming mummies.

Advancements were made in **architecture** and **engineering** too. The ancient Egyptians built giant stone pyramids, statues, and temples. They also built irrigation canals and dams along the Nile.

Rows of large columns were used in many ancient Egyptian temples.

The ancient Egyptians made a **decimal system** that used seven different symbols. They could add and subtract and do some multiplication and division. They could also do fractions and figure out areas and volumes. However, they had no symbol for zero.

The ancient Egyptians used mathematics for such activities as measuring, building, figuring taxes, and cooking.

Can you figure out the numbers these symbols stand for?

The answers are on page 16.

The civilization of ancient Egypt was very successful. Many of their advancements influenced civilizations that came after them.

Glossary

architecture *n.* science or art of planning and designing buildings.

civilization *n.* an advanced way of life that usually includes towns, written forms of language, and special kinds of work for people.

decimal system *n.* system of numbering and counting which is based on the number 10 and its multiples

engineering *n.* science, work, or profession of planning, building, or managing engines, machines, roads, bridges, and so on.

fertile *adj.* able to produce good crops easily.

gravity *n.* the natural force that causes objects to move toward the center of Earth

irrigate *v.* to bring a supply of water to a dry area

obelisk *n.* a tapered, four-sided stone pillar with a top shaped like a pyramid, such as the Washington Monument

Answers for page 15: 3,244; 21,237